D0428915

I Am
Honest
by Sarah L. Schuette

Consulting Editor: Gail Saunders-Smith, Ph.D.

Consultant: Madonna Murphy, Ph.D.
Professor of Education,
University of St. Francis, Joliet, Illinois
Author, *Character Education in America's
Blue Ribbon Schools*

Pebble Books

an imprint of Capstone Press
Mankato, Minnesota

Pebble Books are published by Capstone Press
151 Good Counsel Drive, P.O. Box 669, Mankato, Minnesota 56002
http://www.capstone-press.com

1 2 3 4 5 6 07 06 05 04 03 02

Library of Congress Cataloging-in-Publication Data
Schuette, Sarah L., 1976–
  I am honest / by Sarah L. Schuette.
    p. cm.—(Character values)
  Summary: Simple text and photographs show various ways children can
be honest.
  Includes bibliographical references and index.
  ISBN 0-7368-1440-X (hardcover)
  1. Honesty—Juvenile literature. [1. Honesty.] I. Title. II. Series.
BJ1533.H7 .S34 2003
179'.9—dc21   2001008183

Note to Parents and Teachers

The Character Values series supports national social studies standards for units on citizenship. This book describes honesty and illustrates ways students can be honest. The images support early readers in understanding the text. The repetition of words and phrases helps early readers learn new words. This book also introduces early readers to subject-specific vocabulary words, which are defined in the Words to Know section. Early readers may need assistance to read some words and to use the Table of Contents, Words to Know, Read More, Internet Sites, and Index/Word List sections of the book.

Table of Contents

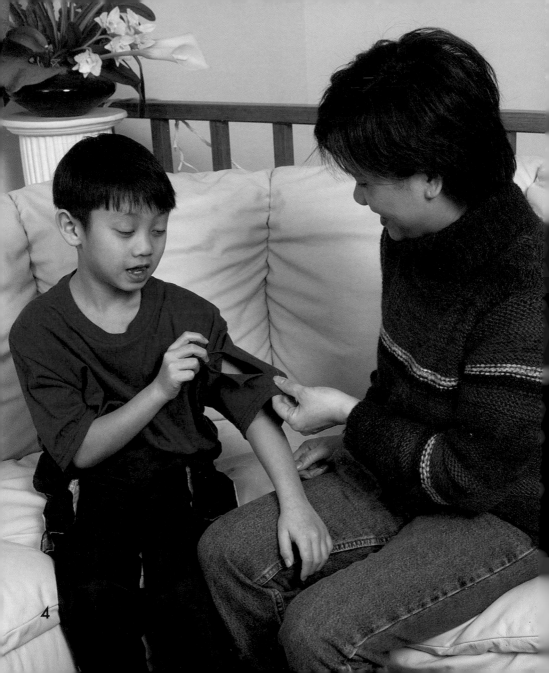

4

I am honest. I tell the truth.

No food or drink allowed in the store

*Thanks for your cooperation
--Management*

I am honest when I follow the rules.

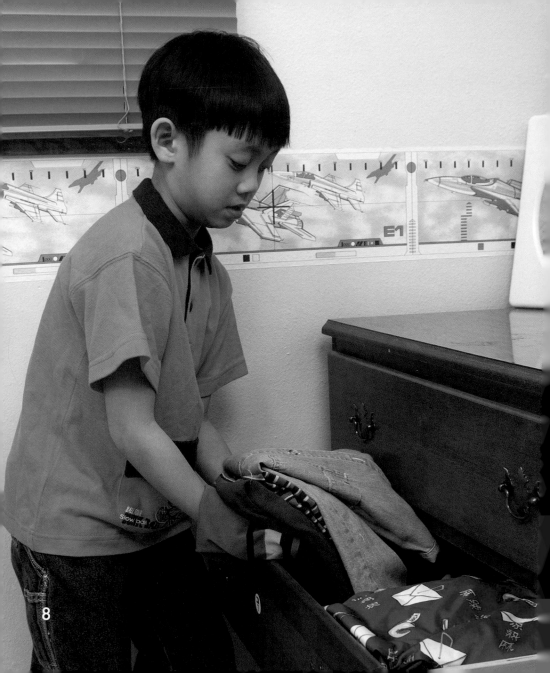

I am honest when I
do what I say I will do.

I pay for the things I want. I tell the clerk if I get too much change.

I do my own work.
I do not copy from
other people.

I tell my friend
if I break his things.

I do not blame others for my mistakes.

I am honest with my parents. I tell them when I am afraid or upset.

I am honest. I tell the truth. People can trust me.

Words to Know

blame—to hold yourself or someone else responsible for something that happened; people who are honest take responsibility for their own actions.

clerk—a person who sells things at a store

copy—to take another person's work and use it as your own

follow—to obey a rule; people are honest when they follow rules.

honest—to be truthful; people who are honest do not lie.

mistake—something that often happens by accident; people do not mean to make mistakes.

rule—an instruction telling people what to do; rules help people learn, stay healthy, and stay safe.

Read More

Althea. *Telling the Truth.* Exploring Emotions. Milwaukee: Gareth Stevens, 1998.

Kyle, Kathryn. *Honesty.* Wonder Books. Chanhassen, Minn.: Child's World, 2002.

Raatma, Lucia. *Honesty.* Character Education. Mankato, Minn.: Bridgestone Books, 2000.

Snyder, Margaret. *Honesty.* Do the Right Thing! Vero Beach, Fla.: Rourke, 1999.

Internet Sites

Character Counts National Home Page
http://www.charactercounts.org

Honesty
http://library.thinkquest.org/J001709/thinkquest
_values/6honesty/honesty_frameset.html

KidsHealth for Kids: Cheating
http://kidshealth.org/kid/feeling/school/
cheating.html

Index/Word List

Word Count: 99
Early-Intervention Level: 9

Credits

Mari C. Schuh, editor; Jennifer Schonborn, series designer and illustrator;
Gary Sundermeyer, photographer; Nancy White, photo stylist; Karen Risch,
product planning editor

Pebble Books thanks the Le family of Mankato, Minnesota, for modeling
in this book.

The author dedicates this book to the memory of her grandparents, Willmar and
Janet Schuette, formerly of Belle Plaine, Minnesota.